# Hidden Beneath the Tides

## UK Marine Special Areas of Conservation

**UK Marine**
SACs Project

Hidden Beneath the Tides
UK Marine Special Areas of Conservation

The UK marine SACs Project is a joint venture involving English Nature (lead agency), Scottish Natural Heritage, Countryside Council for Wales, Environment and Heritage Service Northern Ireland, Joint Nature Conservation Committee and the Scottish Association of Marine Science, with financial support from the European Commission's LIFE Nature Programme.

This booklet was produced with the support of the European Commission's LIFE Nature Programme and published by the UK marine SACs Project, English Nature, Peterborough on behalf of Scottish Natural Heritage, Countryside Council for Wales, Environment and Heritage Service, Department of the Environment for Northern Ireland, Joint Nature Conservation Committee and the Scottish Association of Marine Science.

ISBN 1 85716 579 9
Joint copyright (text only) EN, SNH, CCW, EHS (NI), JNCC & SAMS - October 2001

Additional copies of this report can be obtained by contacting:
The Enquiry Service, English Nature, Northminster House, Peterborough. PE1 1UA
email: enquiries@english-nature.org.uk  Web Site: www.ukmarinesac.org.uk
Phone 01733 455100 Fax 01733 455103
Catalogue code IN7.2

# Contents

**The UK has a vast coastline and a history as a seafaring nation, but even so, we have taken our seas and shoreline for granted. Today, people are realising the value of the colourful and intriguing underwater wildlife around our islands. Where else would you find pens that burrow and glow in the dark, a cucumber that can walk, cannibalistic stars or slugs in frilly nighties?**

In 1992, the Rio Earth Summit brought together the nations of the world in the realisation that the incredible wildlife and resources of our world need special protection and sensitive management if people and planet are to have a future. We are beginning to find that the oceans cannot sustain being used as a giant rubbish dump, neither can they maintain their abundant wildlife if we destroy habitats or persist in over-harvesting vital parts of the food chain.

Following the Summit, the nations of Europe have launched the European Habitats Directive, which aims to ensure that the amazing diversity of Europe's wildlife has a future. One of the ways in which the UK is fulfiling this aim is to set up, for the first time ever, a network of protected marine areas around our coasts to safeguard important species and their habitats. This presents a new and exciting conservation challenge.

*Sunstar and dead man's fingers*

*Featherstar and starfish*

*The Isles of Scilly*

# What is a marine Special Area of Conservation?

Across Europe, Special Areas of Conservation (SACs) are being established on both land and in coastal waters in response to the Habitats Directive. These are some of Europe's most precious wildlife sites, supporting rare, endangered or vulnerable plants and animals or outstanding examples of particular wildlife habitats. Where the designated area includes sea or seashore, it is described as a marine Special Area of Conservation.

In the UK so far, some seventy marine Special Areas of Conservation have been selected by the nature conservation agencies (Scottish Natural Heritage, Countryside Council for Wales, Environment and Heritage Service, Department of the Environment for Northern Ireland, English Nature and Joint Nature Conservation Committee). Together with other statutory bodies, these agencies are working together to learn more about the UK's marine wildlife and how human activities might affect it. They also aim to raise general awareness of the value of marine SACs and the ways in which they will be safeguarded, whilst also recognising the economic, cultural, social and recreational needs of local communities.

This booklet will introduce you to some of the marine habitats and species protected as Special Areas of Conservation under the Habitats Directive. These SAC's will be the first step in protecting the rich and varied life found in some of the most amazing marine areas around the UK.

If you thought our underwater world was murky and lifeless, roll up your trouserlegs, wade into the booklet and prepare yourself for a surprise!

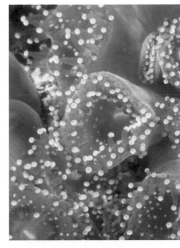

*Jewel anemones*

*Sea fan*

*Dead man's fingers*

Introduction

5

## Fish Eye's View

In the cold waters around our coasts where land meets sea lie magical seascapes, where life in a fluid world is full of danger. If you were a fish, you would be suspended in water. Think for a moment about what this means. In place of breezes and gales you would feel the effect of tides and currents. Salt water would be everywhere, flowing through your mouth and gills and passing through your body and skin. Within a mouthful of water would be a soup of millions of animal and plant plankton. The water would also teem with spawn, eggs and hatchlings released by seaweeds and sea creatures of all shapes and sizes. You might follow the waves as they foam in and claim the shoreline from the birds, feeling with your mouth or whisker-like barbels for worms, shrimps or shellfish amongst the granules of mud or sand.

The 'flowers' in your meadows would be beautiful but dangerous animals, armed with barbed stinging tentacles. Shoals of larger fish and huge flocks of birds would see you as a quick meal. You could shelter amidst forests of tall seaweeds but here too you might meet predators as large as a hungry seal. You would sense sounds from miles away and the pounding of wave against rock would send shockwaves through your body.

Your city might be the reef, where many species crowd together to take advantage of the nooks and crannies or seek a quick snack amongst the crowds. At night in the sea, if you move, you are startled by the flickering torches and street lights which suddenly turn on as tiny luminescent plankton start to glimmer all around you. In the wake of boats, the vast number of shimmering creatures creates what looks like a steady glow!

*'Where the land meets the sea'*

*Small mouthed wrasse*

*Beautifully patterned ballan wrasse*

Amongst the underwater cities, forests, meadows and dunes rove all sorts of many-legged, single-footed and legless animals in an amazing variety of shapes and sizes. Some are heavily armoured, others camouflaged or flamboyantly coloured. Prawns bury themselves in a flurry of legs while starfish move slowly but determinedly on many tiny tentacles on the undersides of their arms. Fragile and graceful, 'feather-stars' avoid being smashed by the waves by keeping to muddy sea bottoms, while jellyfish survive turbulent waters by becoming almost as fluid as water itself.

If you were a newly hatched fish your chances of a long life would be minuscule. If you were born in the sheltered shallows of a fish nursery amongst eelgrass you might, however, stay hidden until you had grown large. If your kidneys could cope with great fluctuations in saltiness you could seek refuge in an estuary or lagoon but might face heightened dangers from pollution. As a large fish you might leave the shores and strike out for the open seas, but even here you are not safe. Watch out for larger predators such as humans, land mammals turned fishermen!

*Colourful male cuckoo wrasse*

*Moon jellyfish are easily recognised by their four coloured rings*

*Firework anemone*

7

# The Hidden World of Sea Caves

*Intertidal sea cave*

**Sea caves can seem primeval, frightening places; wet, dark and worlds away from familiar 'man-made' landscapes. Yet, they are magic doorways between solid rock, and the creatures that live in them are weirdly beautiful.**

## Shapes and forms

Our islands have the most varied and extensive sea caves on the Atlantic coast of Europe. They appear where surging waves have broken in at a weak spot in solid rock. Some are hollows in chalk or limestone. Others slice narrowly into the land, following lines of weakness where millions of years ago rock was forced into upright layers by colliding continents.

## Dark deeds and hidden treasure

Tales are told of smugglers hiding their contraband in shoreline caves. There is much truth in this, but in shallower caves any tubs or barrels would have been smashed to pieces in the surf, so goods were stored in the sand or anchored beneath the surface.

## Stranger than legend

So how does life survive the dashing waves? Many amazing animals cling on to existence against the odds. Some wear armour. Some use their own guy ropes. Others bore into rock or cling on with suckers.

*'But that was nothing to
what things came out
From the sea-caves of
Criccieth yonder.'
'What were they?
Mermaids? dragons? ghosts?'
'Nothing at all
of any things like that.'
'What were they then?'
　　'All sorts of queer things.
Things never seen or heard or
written about...'*

(From 'Welsh Incident' by Robert Graves)

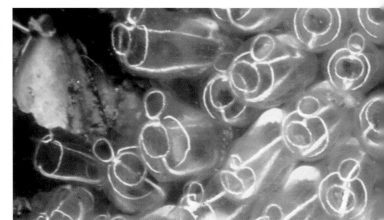

*Lightbulb sea squirts*

# Life in intertidal sea caves

As the tide rushes in, it brings with it boulders and pebbles which scour the walls of intertidal sea caves until they are smooth. When it rushes out, the cave is left high and dry. Life is harsh for animals living here. Even if you are a sea anemone that can live for many years, you must pick your spot carefully to avoid being swept away or crushed by a swirling mass of water and rocks.

When exploring intertidal sea caves, people often find groups of creatures divided into clear bands or zones according to how they have evolved to cope with varying levels of battering and exposure (see Reefs, page 32).

## On the threshold

In submerged cave mouths, sponges and colonial sea squirts thrive on passing titbits in the turbulence by sucking in water and filtering out tiny food particles. Pretty anemones inject venom into larger prey with thousands of spring-loaded, barbed harpoons concealed within their tentacles.

## Into the unknown

Deeper inside, barnacles survive the drier times by battening down the hatches and waiting for the next tide. Colonies of tinier creatures called sea moss live as lacy, mat-like crusts or form miniature forests hanging upside-down from overhangs.

Right at the back in darker, drier conditions, grey seals give birth on rocky ledges or patches of sand.

*'Baked bean' sea squirt and anemones on cave walls*

*Dog whelks, topshells and barnacles*

*Inside a sea cave*

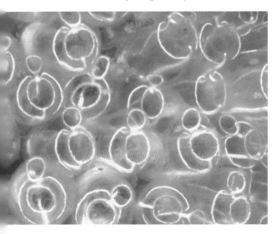

# The mysteries of subtidal sea caves

Dangerous, but irresistible to the adventurous is the underwater sea cave, full of living surprises, tough enough to withstand the ocean yet fragile enough to be harmed by a diver's bubbles.

*Curled octopus*

## Going with the flow

If a subtidal cave forms a tunnel, the waves flow through freely, bringing with them a feast of minute plankton particles which sweep into the clutches of brightly coloured filter feeders – sponges and solitary sea squirts. These animals form a spectacular garden over the cave walls. Many are actually dark-loving deep water species.

## Feel the beat

In a blind-ended cave incoming waves are forced to come to a stop as they hit the water already inside. The compression of these waves at the cave entrance causes booming shock waves which feel to a diver 'like a drum beating right next to your lung'.

## Wildlife in the chasms

Seals often swim in sea caves, their cries echoing eerily in the dark. Only underwater do you appreciate their true grace and beauty as they twist and turn, swoop and spin.

Lobsters and crabs hide in small holes in the rocks where they feel protected.

*Common lobster*

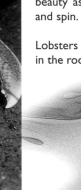

*Common seal*

## Plants or animals?

Plants need light to survive, so the brightly coloured 'weeds' in sea caves are not what they seem. Red-coloured seaweeds do manage to survive in poor light, but the flowers of the dark recesses are actually predatory animals. The common names of many cave wall species describe their plant-like appearance. There are dahlia anemones, sea moss, sea firs and gooseberry sea squirts. All these animals spend the first few days or weeks of life swirling around in the currents as tiny, free-swimming larvae in the planktonic 'soup' before finding a permanent home on a roof or wall.

## What is a sponge?

Sponges often look more like delicate seaweeds than bath sponges. They are the most primitive multi-celled animals in the world. They draw water in through fine holes in their body walls, extracting oxygen and minute food particles, then sending the water out again through a larger hole.

*Dahlia anemone*

*Cave community of jewel anemones and sponges*

*Pink volcano sponge*

## Jewels of the sea

The brightly coloured jewel anemones are soft corals which often clump together in the safety of an overhang.
Other beauties include scarlet and gold star-coral and cup corals.

# Havens of Wildlife

**Most of us love to visit the sea. What could be more relaxing than sitting on the sun-drenched shores of a bay listening to frothy waves dragging sand and pebbles back and forth? Beyond the headlands the open sea stretches far away, mistily mingling with the horizon. But what life is there in the wide waters of the bay?**

Bays support a stunning variety and abundance of marine life. Within them can be found saltmarshes, sandbanks, mudflats, reefs and all the life that comes with them.

The most familiar inlet is a pocket sized ocean contained within a curve of land between rocky headlands, quite sheltered but flushed out twice a day by the tide. In the centre of the bay the beach absorbs the force of the waves.

Another type of inlet is a shallow basin connected to the sea by a low, rocky ledge. These occur in Western Scotland and Northern Ireland and are rarely found elsewhere in Europe. We also have drowned river valleys formed after the last Ice Age, when ancient river valleys that had been scoured or deepened by glaciers were flooded by rising sea levels.

*The stranded fragment*
*of ocean rippled*
*While far away*
*beyond the huge boulders*
*The blue sea rumbled*
*and roared its voices*
*Making me scream out loud*
*with infant joy*

*From 'Giant's steps' by Ian Heard*

Busy day at the beach

Red cushion star and Bloody Henry starfish

*Sea squirts*

# Life in the washing machine

Currents and tides have a great influence upon both habitats and wildlife in shallow bays. Most bays are sheltered from the full impact of the waves, so their floors are covered in soft sands or silts. Here you will find burrowing anemones, sea pens, starfish and a host of shellfish, some which live between two shell-halves like castanets and others curled inside shells shaped into elegant spirals and swirls.

If tides rush in forcefully, the sand will be clean, rocks will be exposed and coated with creatures such as sea squirts and sponges that filter their food from the water.

*Top shell*

*The scallop is protected by two shell-halves*

*Tidal rapids, Cuan Sound, Western Isles*

13

# Survival in the bay

In the waters of the bay all may appear calm, but beneath the surface there is a continual struggle for survival using weird and wonderful attack and defence strategies.

Glossy necklace shells prey on other shellfish. They soften the shell with a chemical before drilling a neat hole through it and eating the animal inside. Lampreys feed on living fish. Vampire-like, they clasp onto the skin of their prey, rasping through it and sucking out the blood.

The largest British sea cucumber, known as the cotton spinner, is a master of self defence. Not only does it look spiky and difficult to eat, it can also tangle attackers by throwing cotton-like threads from its back end which are sticky enough to wrap around a man's hand and hold it shut. Other sea cucumbers burrow, which is also the strategy of a potato-shaped urchin called the heart urchin, whose spines are soft and fold inwards when it buries itself in the sand.

*Sea slug feeding on sea mat*

Sea slugs graze on other animals such as anemones, feather-like hydroids and sponges. They can be many different colours, often closely matching the colour of the animals they eat. Many sea slugs have colourful gills that resemble the stinging tentacles of anemones. This may help deter predators.

The slug-like vegetarian sea hares confuse their attackers by squirting a purple dye at them.

Hermit crabs have no shell of their own. They protect their soft bodies by borrowing empty shells from other creatures, often sharing them with marine worms on the inside and predatory anemones on the outside.

*Hermit crab*

# Light and colour in the bay

Light plays a vital part in creating the rich life found in the UK's shallow bays. Where sunlight can penetrate to the sea floor, plants can grow. Those that can root in sand, particularly eelgrass, are very important to the structure of the seabed as they trap silt, creating sandbanks and mudbanks (see Estuaries and Submerged Sandbanks sections). Seaweeds attach themselves to rocks, shells or other seaweeds. All are algae, but underwater they can look like mermaids' tresses, the folds of a silken gown, or even shoelaces and belts.

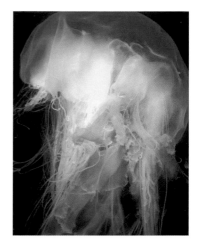

Lion's mane jellyfish look like translucent, violet parasols as they pulse through the water trailing their frilly tentacles.

*Sea slug*

## Colourful animals

In the sea, animals and even some worms – can outdo plants when it comes to bright colours and delicate beauty. The peacock worm lives under the sand in a tube, but sports a beautiful fan of delicate tentacles which sift the water for food particles and oxygen.

Diving or going on a trip in a glass-bottomed boat enables people exploring shallow bays to see at first hand vivid colours and fascinating forms which are usually swathed in the darkness of the deep oceans. You might have the added bonus of seeing sea otters or larger mammals like seals, dolphins or the harbour porpoise coming in to feed (see page 38).

*King scallop*

*Peacock worms*

# Powerhouses of Energy Production

As rivers widen out towards the sea, fresh water mingles with salt water surging in on the tide. Here, water and land come together, creating sandbanks, mudflats and saltmarshes. The UK has 150 estuaries – more than any other European country – and their sheer variety is unrivalled. Like rainforests and coral reefs, they are among the most productive ecosystems on earth.

The water in estuaries is layered like a fluid sandwich. Fresh water at the top flows towards the sea, heavier salt water at the bottom flows in and out with the tide, and brackish water – a mixture of the two – moves to and fro in between. Even the sandbanks and mudflats are constantly shifting in the currents.

## A busy place

The pungent sea air carries a symphony of estuary sounds – the honking of geese, the penetrating alarm calls of the redshank, the high-pitched, musical cry of the curlew accompanied by the gentler whistles of the wigeon. There are human noises too. Most of the UK's major ports are on estuaries. Boats ply up and down alongside yachts and windsurfers. Estuaries have also been harbours, waste dumps and places to claim for development and farmland.

*Industry on the shoreline*

*Afon Mawddach – shifting sands and mud*

## Food, glorious food

Rich sediments washed downriver and stirred up from the seabed are the key to an estuary's fertility. They contain tiny plant particles and microscopic animals in the mud which fuel an elaborate food chain. The organic matter feeds billions of tiny worms, shrimps and snails. These are snapped up by many millions of larger, predatory worms which in turn are the staple diet of many thousands of fish and seabirds.

## Where soil meets sediment

Estuaries blur the boundary between land and sea. Along their edges, a small number of plants which can survive in brackish waters slowly establish saltmarshes, a mosaic of very special plants and animals. The first to colonise the bare mud are tough cord grass or fleshy glassworts which are able to withstand the salty conditions by storing fresh water in their leaves. Their roots trap sediment and so the saltmarsh grows.

Eelgrass grows on sandy-muddy estuary shores, trapping silt as well as feeding a large proportion of the entire world population of overwintering brent geese. During the summer, saltmarshes may be used as grazing land for livestock such as cattle and sheep.

Beyond the reach of all but the highest tides, saltmarsh grasses and rushes grow alongside sea blite and the pretty, pale purple sea aster. In May thrift turns the marshes pink, and in summer sea-lavender creates a mauve haze reminiscent of heather moorland.

*Sea lavender*

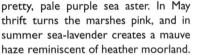
*Samphire*

*Cord grass – a pioneer plant of saltmarshes*

*Curlew*

# Superfish

*'Water, water, everywhere
Nor any drop to drink.'*
(From 'The Ancient Mariner' by S.T. Coleridge)

Coleridge is referring to our inability to survive on seawater. Most fish cannot survive in both sea water and fresh water. However, a few remarkable species do leave the sea and swim far up estuaries to freshwater rivers and streams.

## Upstream and downstream

The salmon is one of these remarkable species. Salmons' lives begin in freshwater, in the upper reaches of rivers. After the young fish have hatched and grown to a few centimetres in length, they head down river into the estuary. Here they stay until they have adapted to the salty water and are ready to swim out to sea.

During their life at sea salmon grow very rapidly. In two years they can grow from just a few grams in weight to as much as 6kg. After several years, the fish may swim over thousands of kilometres of ocean before returning to the river of their birth. How they find their way back is still a mystery, but it is thought that they may be able to recognise the smell and taste of the water from their particular river. Once again, the salmon spend some time in the estuary whilst their bodies undergo dramatic changes so they can survive in fresh water. They then battle their way far upriver where they lay their eggs, completing one generation's life-cycle and beginning the next.

The beginning of the amazing life-cycle of the eel was a mystery until recently, when it was found that the adults spawn far away in the Sargasso Sea. As tiny, transparent larvae sometimes called 'glassfish' they drift to our coast on a sea current called the Gulf Stream. There they transform into elvers, miniature versions of adult eels, and begin swimming up estuaries towards fresh water where they mature. They are tolerant of pollution as well as varying salinity, and can even slither short distances across land.

*Common eel*

*Curlew probing
for a lugworm*

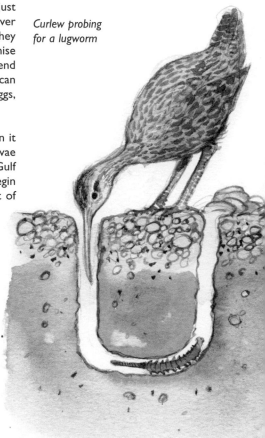

*Leaping salmon*

# Ocean incomers

Flounder are a species of flatfish that breed in the sea and feed on cockles and marine worms. However, these lopsided-looking fish can also tolerate very low salinities and may swim up estuaries to the lower reaches of rivers where they eat insect larvae, snails, crustaceans and worms.

Shoals of bass and mullet can survive in estuaries, along with three-spined sticklebacks, gobies and lampreys. Ocean fish such as cod and plaice use the sheltered sandbanks and mudflats of the saltier areas as nurseries for their young.

*Left: flounder*

*Oystercatcher foraging for shellfish*

# Birds of a feather

Even if you just glimpse an estuary from a car or train you will notice countless birds on exposed areas of sand and mud. Most are migrants whose lives depend upon these soggy service stations. Visitors en route from the Arctic include swans, geese, ducks and hundreds of thousands of waders. The pattern of their daily lives mirrors the tide's ebb and flow, with vast, scattered flocks feeding at low water and roosting at high water.

Each species of bird is adapted to its own diet, so large numbers of different species can live together. Wide-billed ducks like scaup dive for snails, while the red-breasted merganser uses its serrated bill to grip fish. Redshank and oystercatcher stab for burrowing shellfish, while the curlew probes deeper for ragworms and snails.

*The shelduck is dependent upon estuaries, feeding mainly upon the laver spire shell, a small but abundant mud snail*

*Common terns*

# Buried Treasure

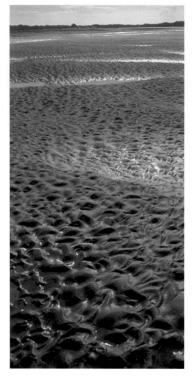

When the tide retreats from a stretch of coastline you may find yourself gazing at an expanse of golden sand or glistening mud. At first glance these tide-rippled, relatively featureless surfaces might seem lifeless, but as any sea bird might tell you, a little digging and probing will reveal a wealth of living treasure.

Mudflats have been undervalued in the past and many have been lost, drained or reclaimed for agriculture and industry. They are, however, an important wildlife habitat in estuaries and bays and a vital natural sea defence for the open coast. Threatened further by rising sea levels, now is the time to appreciate their wonders and investigate their inhabitants.

*Rippled muddy sand*

*Mudflats are an important wildlife habitat*

## Life in the soup

Whilst mud may look solid, the upper layer may be almost 90% water. Further down there is little oxygen, just foul-smelling black mud. Despite such harsh conditions, a few shellfish such as cockles, razorshells and peppery furrow shells manage to survive here by making a vertical channel like a snorkel, down which they pump fresh sea water.

## Living in sand

*Cockle*

Living conditions in sand depend on how long you are underwater. Near the high tide mark only strong-limbed, armour-plated shrimp and wood-louse-like animals survive by breathing air, scavenging, scuttling, wriggling or hopping and hiding in seaweed or under stones.

Further down the shore, worms and delicate shellfish lie buried and out of sight. Cockles and tellins shut up shop when the tide goes out, trapping water in their shells so they do not dry out. Twice a day when the incoming tide brings them fresh supplies of food they open their shells to feed.

Lugworms live in U-shaped burrows in wet, muddy sand. They eat the bacteria found on sand grains, leaving curly casts like walnut whips along the beach. They are a crucial food to birds and fish, especially waders and flatfish.

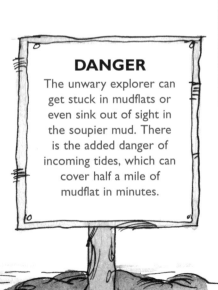

### DANGER

The unwary explorer can get stuck in mudflats or even sink out of sight in the soupier mud. There is the added danger of incoming tides, which can cover half a mile of mudflat in minutes.

*Lugworm casts*

*Sandflats at Afon Mawddach*

# Monsters of the mud

It's not science fiction, there really are monsters lurking in the mud. Large carnivorous catworms have fearsome extending jaws. They use them to dig and to grab other worms and shellfish, which they hunt with rapid, determined wiggles.

Equally formidable are the dangerous but beautiful turquoise and orange ragworms. When they are agitated, they project an egg-shaped weapon from their mouths, armed with a pair of strong teeth and scattered smaller teeth. These jaws are used for attack and defence, and can bite the fingers of bait-diggers!

Ancient, primitive worms without segments slide through the mud too, hiding under any stones. An unbelievably stretchy, ribbon-shaped animal called the bootlace worm is a vigorous hunter of bristle worms such as the lugworm. It might be up to ten metres long but specimens of up to 30 metres have been recorded!

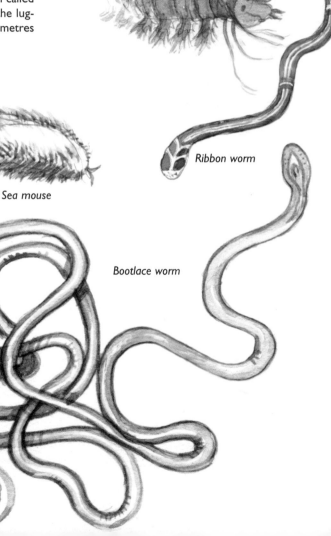

*Top: head of king ragworm*
*Below: common ragworm*

*Candy stripe and spotted flatworms*

*Sea mouse*

*Ribbon worm*

*Bootlace worm*

# Fast food

*She wheeled her wheelbarrow*
*Through streets broad and narrow*
*Crying "Cockles and mussels! alive, alive, oh"*
(From 'Cockles and mussels', traditional song)

The large worms and shellfish in the mud and sand are just the tip of the iceberg. Millions of tiny worms and snails and unimaginable numbers of single-celled plants and animals live hidden from view, turning energy from the sun and minute nutrient particles into food for a chain of ever-larger animals.

Huge flocks of migrating birds such as dunlin and knot depend on these mud and sandscapes to supply them with high energy food as they refuel along their astonishingly long journeys. Other birds such as the redshank and oystercatcher rely on them all year round. They are exploited by humans too. Cockles teem close to the surface, harvested by some people with rakes and tractors. The larger lugworms and ragworms are dug for bait in their thousands. Flat and soggy they may be, but these muds and sands, packed with amazing inhabitants, are some of the richest habitats on the planet.

*Knot*

*Harvesting cockles*

# Life in the Shifting Sand

**Submerged sandbanks have been a hazard for unwary sailors throughout history, but a bounty for fishermen. Tide-swept or tranquil they can be carpeted in maerl – a plant that creates coral-like reefs – or covered in the extensive areas of eelgrass, the only flowering plant to live in the sea around our coasts.**

## Living in a dynamic environment

Incoming tides swirl around and over submerged sandbanks, washing away mud and leaving coarser sand or gravel behind. They constantly change shape as channels are carved, filled, and re-carved in the sand of estuaries and bays.

Little can live in this maelstrom of moving sand grains, but some creatures survive on the surface. Scallops make a slight dent in the gravelly sediment and sit with their curved side down, almost disappearing altogether. They have a curious beard of tentacles around the margins of their shells, which helps them sense passing food. They stay motionless for long periods of time, but if they are startled will swim away backwards, opening and shutting their shells like a runaway set of false teeth.

*Good heavens! Here comes my wife, all in tears, pointing out to me a poor ship, just tumbled over on a sandbank on the Cumberland Coast. Moments are precious (say the people on the beach), the flood runs at ten miles an hour.*

*(From a letter by Thomas Carlyle, Scottish historian and sociological writer)*

*The queen scallop's light sensitive 'eyes' look out for predators*

24

The strange-looking brittlestars catch food by raising spindly tentacles into the current, reaching for passing morsels. Where currents are strong, they manage to avoid being swept away by linking arms and forming a living mat, which can totally obscure the seabed. By helping each other to hold on they have more free legs available for catching food.

## To build or to dig?

The waves and currents of the sea can stir up sediments from the sea bottom making it murky, blocking the light and damaging delicate gills. The best thing to do in such conditions is to burrow or build.

## Builders in the sand

Sandmason worms build tubes from sand grains, making delicate branching structures that resemble bare trees in winter. Other tubeworms create finely crafted cones like Alpine horns or flexible, worm-shaped tubes so numerous that they can hold large areas of sand firmly together.

The honeycomb reefworm finds safety in numbers and builds massive honeycomb structures from hundreds of tubes. Up to 1700 worms, each 3.5cm long, can live in a square metre of the colony. These humpy reefs can provide protection for animals such as shrimps and a stable home for anemones.

*A living mat of brittlestars*

*Sandmason worms*

*Honeycomb reefworm*

25

# Sand burrowers

Sand eels are expert burrowers and a staple food for diving birds such as puffins, razor-bills and terns and fish such as cod, mackerel and herring. Their pointed lower jaw and narrow shape helps them disappear quickly into the sand. They swim in large shoals with their heads pointed downwards, ready to take cover at the first sign of danger. Unfortunately they cannot hide from people. Harvesting sand eels on a massive scale for fishmeal is having a drastic effect on their numbers, and a knock-on effect upon the birds and fish which rely on them for food.

Flatfish nestle amongst the sand grains in disguise, looking like an ordinary piece of seabed until they move away with a flurry. Soft sand in these more sheltered places is also home to less mobile animals, such as burrowing sea anemones and waving sea pens. Some sea pens emit flashes or pulses of brilliant light, looking like glowing pen quills, and can withdraw into their permanent tubes if disturbed.

*A slender sea pen*

*A swimming crab hides in the sand*

*Cut-away section of a subtidal sandbank*

# When the sand does not shift

Sandbanks are not always places of shifting sands. In some places the sandy seabed can be quite static and it is here that eelgrass and maerl grow. These two different plants both benefit wildlife by providing homes and shelter for a host of other creatures.

## Maerl, the 'coral' seaweed

Maerl is a term for a group of incredible organisms, which might fool you in a game of animal, vegetable, mineral. These free-living seaweeds colonise sandbanks where there is clear, unpolluted water combined with tidal movements, like many of the sea lochs of Scotland. They are incredibly slow growing, building a coral-like skeleton from calcium extracted from seawater. This may grow by only 1mm every year. Their random, hedgehog shapes form dense, brittle reefs, which dramatically increase the diversity of wildlife on the sea floor. Their labyrinth of nooks and crannies are perfect for housing shrimps, crabs, fish and many other plants and animals, some of which are unique to maerl beds.

In some places maerl is harvested by people. It is dredged up from the seabed and ground into a fine powder, which is used as a conditioner for acid soils or roasted to make quick lime.

*Eelgrass with snakelocks anemone*

*Velvet swimming crab sheltering in maerl*

# Surviving in Isolation

*Foxtail stonewort*

**Saline lagoons are unique water worlds – salty yet barely connected to the sea. If you were a gull flying overhead you would see them as patches of shallow water set slightly apart, separated from the open ocean by barriers of shingle, sand or rock.**

They can appear as tranquil havens whose crystal clear waters shimmer with tantalising glimpses of the world below. Or they may seem hostile and forbidding, wave rippled and windswept with no indication of the life they contain. Either way they are very special places, a rare and endangered habitat that is often threatened by pollution, damage and industrial development.

*The Fleet Lagoon bordered by Chesil Bank*

# Hidden stresses

Lagoons may look idyllic, but the wildlife that lives in them faces hidden challenges, as conditions can change dramatically.

The most important condition that can change is salinity. Lagoons may become almost as salty as the sea after a big storm, or be diluted to freshwater by heavy rains. On still, summer days the water may be crystal clear, and rare plants such as stoneworts can thrive. But then wind, pollution and industrial development can turn the water cloudy, which makes life hard for lagoon plants. Lastly, the temperature of the water can change. It may be as warm as a bath in summer, or cold enough to freeze in winter.

*Lagoons come in many shapes and sizes*

*Right: the upward curving bill of the avocet scythes the water to filter out small creatures*

*Swimmers beware! Lagoons can be colder than the nearby sea*

*Underwater eelgrass meadows*

# Curious creatures

Lagoon waters teem with unusual wildlife, some of it very small and much of it unique. Hidden from view are myriad hoards of minute snails, each adapted to a different way of life. Some live at the water's edge, burrowing into the bank. Others live on seagrass, seaweed, in mud, or on rock.

Seagrasses in the lagoon are home to other peculiar animals. There is the rare eelgrass sea fir, a colony of hundreds of tiny translucent animals called hydroids which grow on the blades of the seagrass. These intricate colonies look like plants and are eaten by the lagoon sea slug, a graceful, frilly white animal, which looks like an angel as it swims. Other curious creatures found only in lagoons are the trembling sea mat and the lagoon sandworm.

One of the smallest animals to be found in lagoons is perhaps the rarest and most remarkable. The colourless starlet sea anemone grows to only 1.5cm high. It lives part buried in fine mud or attached to plants, where it traps unwary snails and shrimps for food. All the starlet sea anemones found in the UK are female and are clones of one original animal, regardless of their location.

## Plants of salt and shallows

The unusual stoneworts, such as the foxtail stonewort, are a highly specialised family adapted to life in lagoons. They rely on a steady supply of salts found in the concentrated lagoon water, which they use to strengthen their leaves and stems. They feel hard and brittle to the touch.

*The rare starlet sea anemone*

Different plants inhabit different parts of lagoons. Dozens of different seaweeds thrive in the brackish water found near areas often inundated by the sea. These are replaced by pondweeds and reeds further inland around freshwater inlets. In summer, however, the whole lagoon can be smothered in a layer of hairy-looking algae, which floats up and down with the tide.

*Foxtail stonewort in 'flower'*

*Lagoon sea slug*

# Lagoon visitors

Not all the inhabitants of lagoons are there to stay. They provide sheltered feeding and roosting sites for many uncommon and distinctive birds including avocets, little terns, wigeon and the pure white little egret.

Shoals of young marine fish benefit from the shelter and rich pickings to eat. They are quite happy to be stranded in the lagoon for a while, left behind after storms or very high tides. One such fish is the mullet, whose comb-fringed lips skim the seabed for microscopic plants and mud animals. Mullet can cope with changes in salinity and often manage to swim upstream where the water contains very little salt.

Bass are also quite content in a lagoon, and can tolerate totally fresh water. Sleek and silver, they can grow to a metre long, but the younger individuals in the lagoon shoals are a tenth of this size.

*Wigeon – lagoon visitors*

*Bass*

*Butterfish*

# An Underwater Metropolis

**Picture a reef, and you might well think of tropical corals. But reefs cover many miles of our own shoreline. Although the UK is high in the northern hemisphere, our own reefs are unique, exciting and colourful places too.**

Most of Britain's reefs are made of bedrock or boulders, but you can hardly see the rock for the extraordinary plants and animals that cover them. In strong currents and light, forests of kelp wave like windswept trees on a stormy day. In deeper, darker surges, filigree sea mats, soft corals and sponges trap minute organisms that sweep past. Shallow, sheltered spots look like gardens of delicate seaweeds and anemones. Further down on sheltered reefs, silt and small stones can settle on the rocky seabed, providing hideaways for tubeworms like the beautiful fan worm, and mobile creatures like squat lobsters, wrasse and the fearsome conger eel.

*The world below the brine,*
*Forests at the bottom of the sea,*
*the branches, the leaves,*
*Sea lettuce, vast lichens,*
*strange flowers and seeds,*
*the thick tangle, openings,*
*and pink turf..*

(The World Below the Brine, from 'Leaves of Grass' by Walt Whitman)

## Patterns of life

From rugged shores to dark depths, life on the rocky reef is crammed into horizontal bands as clear as painted stripes, organised according to levels of exposure to sun, wind and tide. The next five pages take you on a journey of discovery down the reef zones from the top of the beach to the dark seabed.

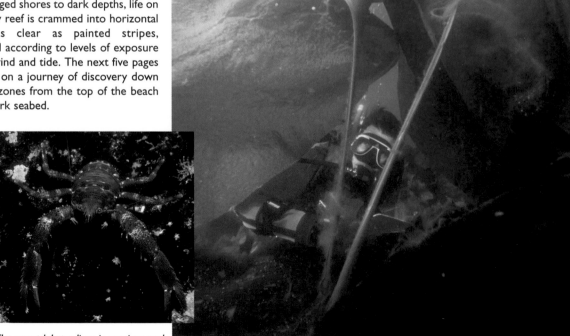

*The squat lobster lives in crevices and comes out to feed at night*

*Diver in a forest of kelp*

# Rocky shore

We begin our journey on a rocky shore. Sometimes underwater, sometimes exposed to the elements, the seashore faces greater extremes than any other environment.

## Upper shore

At the top, facing hours of biting winds or baking sunshine, is the 'splash zone' where contact with the sea is limited to salt spray. In these harsh conditions the rocks are bare apart from colourful lichens which may be as flat as paint splashes. Life is also harsh in nearby rockpools. In hot weather they heat up, becoming stagnant and very salty. In wet weather they fill with rainwater which cannot support sea life.

Some animals survive quite high up the shore. You might find barnacles, limpets and small winkles. The limpet survives the drying effects of the sun by grinding out a hole in the rock, into which it fits exactly. When submerged at high tide its muscular foot pulls it along as it scrapes up algae with a ribbon-like tongue lined with numerous hook-shaped teeth. As the water retreats the limpet returns to its home, clamping itself down. If you are lucky you may see an algae-free trail where it has been.

*The trail left by a grazing limpet*

*An exposed rocky shore*

## Stuck in the middle

The mid-shore has less time to dry out between tides. In exposed areas, beds of mussels join the limpets and barnacles. Where the rocks are more sheltered, wrack seaweeds begin to take hold, some with air-filled bladders like bubble wrap. Even seaweeds that grow underwater need light to grow and the bladders help them float sky-wards when the tide comes in. The wracks provide moist shelter for beadlet anemones and dog whelks.

Like the limpet, the dog whelk has a long tongue called a radula, but despite its innocent appearance this familiar whelk is a driller killer. It uses its radula to pierce the armour of barnacles or mussels before gruesomely sucking out the contents.

Rockpools are home to gobies, blennies, shannies and the eel-shaped butterfish which graze on small creatures in the pools. These smooth-skinned, surf-tolerant fish can survive out of water under wet seaweed if necessary, but only the very patient observer will catch more than a glimpse of them as they dart for cover.

## Lower shore – survivors in the surf

The lower shore has the richest diversity of plants and animals as it is underwater for long periods of time. Brown and red manes of seaweeds can completely conceal rocks which may be covered with periwinkles. The weed's slimy elasticity deters animals from fastening on to them, which would block out the light they need for photosynthesis. It also protects them from being damaged as they are rubbed together by powerful waves.

When the tide goes out, breadcrumb sponges, dahlia sea anemones, sea squirts and Irish moss seaweed can be found hidden under a moist seaweed blanket of wrack.

*Right: butterfly blenny*

*A slippery butterfish*

*Star sea squirts*

# Forests at sea

From land, the sea looks like nothing but water, but at low tide you might notice strappy oarweeds marking the start of another zone dominated by sturdy seaweeds known as kelp. Kelp grow up towards the light like trees. To a diver, passing through the kelp feels 'like walking into a well-established oak forest'. Living amongst the 'trees' are a wealth of plants and animals.

## Creatures of the forest

The leafy fronds of the canopy are decorated with a coat of feathery sea firs and lacy sea mats which like to feed in strong currents. Formed from colonies of tiny, box-shaped animals with tentacles, sea mats spread several millimetres a day to keep ahead of grazing sea slugs.

Star sea squirts colonise kelp too, clustering together into a star pattern beneath a jelly-like covering. From a distance they look like a patch of orange, yellow, white or blue fungus.

Spiny sea urchins graze underwater amongst the kelps eating small plants and animals such as algae and barnacles. They walk slowly on movable spines and suckered feet and may dominate the bottom of the rocky reef like an army of walking pincushions.

*Tide swept kelp forest and rich reef community with dead man's fingers*

Attaching the kelp to the rocks are holdfasts. Like huge suckers they are branched for a good grip, but unlike roots they are not used to feed the plant. Among the holdfasts hide tiny crabs, predatory worms and brittlestars.

Between the kelp plants, the rocks may be hidden under a thick carpet of red seaweeds, while in tide-swept areas fuzzy dead man's fingers poke up from the seabed.

The blue-rayed limpet feeds on the kelps. Although the animals are only 1–2cm long, they can be so abundant that the holdfast may be eaten right through, causing the kelp to lose its firm grip and topple from the rock. It lives up to its name, with vivid blue stripes adorning its shell.

*Egg wrack*

*Holdfast*

# Underwater meadows

Kelp need plenty of light so thick growths are confined to shallower waters. As the kelp thin, you enter lush, waving meadows of smaller, red seaweeds which can thrive in dimmer conditions. Parting the bushes, you find a world of animals hiding underneath on the rocks.

The solitary Devonshire cup coral is found here even in cold northern waters, pinned to the rock like a stud. It has petal-like tentacles like a sea anemone, but sports a hard, limey skeleton. Covering the rocks is a dense, colourful turf of other small animals such as sponges and sea squirts. Featherstars, common and spiny starfish hunt for molluscs. Spectacular sunstars, which have up to thirteen arms, prey on their five-limbed relatives.

*A colourful turf of reef-dwelling plants and animals*

## The secret garden

As the light fades in deeper water, all is dark and quiet in the final reef zone. You switch on a torch and you are amazed. Hidden in the darkness, the animals beyond the seaweed zone are as colourful as any flower. Colonies of the vividly coloured jewel anemone form flowerbeds of bright green and pink. Sea squirts and sponges form strange and beautiful seascapes. Sea fans, hydroids and fanworms wave tentacles more delicate than any petal.

Carnivores from the shallows are here too. While starfish prise shells open, vividly colourful wrasse crunch them up, shells and all, with their powerful jaws. The skeletal-looking sea spider (named for its eight legs) attaches itself to anemones and sea firs, apparently eating them without being stung.

*A delicate sea fan*

*A garden of anemones and sponges*

*A bright red sunstar*

# Reefs made by animals

Rocks are not the sole reef structures around our shores. The few British corals live alone, but we do have incredible reefs made by other animals whose skeletal homes, like the colonial corals, create a marine metropolis as they build up over the years.

The honeycomb reef worms build tubes made of strongly glued sand grains, attached to anything solid. They live in large colonies, the tubes forming a strong humped mass on lower shore rocks, often half buried in sand. The worms themselves look rather like fancy pink combs.

Serpula tubeworms build hard, bone-like tubes on rocks. More and more tubes can be built upon those of past generations until large reefs are created.

The horse mussel clumps together closely with its neighbours upon the shells of its ancestors. Over thousands of years the dead ones can form a layer several metres thick. The living mussels at the top of the reef are an ideal perch for filter feeders and soft corals.

Sponges, sea squirts, sea fans, anemones and a host of mobile creatures from shrimps to fish will quickly take advantage of any reef-like object, transforming it into a bustling sealife city.

*Mussels feeding*

*Low shore serrated wrack*

*A reef built by honeycomb worms*

*Right: an edible crab nestling with featherstars*

37

# Seals and Dolphins in our Coastal Waters

**Marine Special Areas of Conservation have been designated to protect not only rare, endangered or vulnerable habitats but also threatened species. Of these, marine mammals are many people's favourites. Perhaps this is because, like us, they are warm blooded, intelligent and seem to enjoy playing in the water.**

Many people will be surprised to learn that over 20 species of whale, dolphin and porpoise (known collectively as cetaceans) can be seen around the UK. Boat trips give you a chance for a closer look. Otherwise, there are two species that can often be spotted from the shore, if you are looking in the right place at the right time!

*Bottlenose dolphin with calf*

*'Dynamic duo'*

## Two coastal cetaceans

Bottlenose dolphins are the most wide-spread of all cetaceans, inhabiting almost all the worlds oceans and seas. Gregarious and fun-loving, they live in groups far out to sea, but may also be found closer inshore in bays, harbours and estuaries. The best places to see bottlenose dolphins in the UK are the Moray Firth in Scotland and Cardigan Bay in Wales where they are found all the year round.

*A group of harbour porpoises*

The harbour porpoise is one of the worlds smallest cetaceans and is often found alone or in small groups close to shallow bays or estuaries. Unlike the bottlenose dolphin, they are shy and rarely leap out of the water or play around boats. However, if you are lucky, you may catch a fleeting glimpse of their triangular-shaped fin and hear them exhale before disappearing beneath the water again.

## Seals around our shores

Two species of seal breed in the UK, the grey seal and the common seal. You can tell them apart by their size, head shape and colour.

Grey seals can be huge, with males growing to over 2 metres in length and weighing up to 330kg! They have large roman noses and are usually dark grey or brown, often with blotches, though the pups have soft white fur. Today the UK has over half the world's population of grey seals.

*Common seal*

There are also around 50,000 common seals in the UK. These animals are smaller than the grey seal and have a more rounded, dog-like face. Their colour can vary from pale to dark grey, often with dark spots or rings.

On land, seals may look awkward and clumsy, but they are extremely agile and graceful underwater. They can hold their breath for up to 20 minutes, have been recorded diving down to 300 metres and can swim up to 100km a day. Sometimes they spend several days out at sea, sleeping with their noses bobbing out of the water. Pups can swim and dive when just a few hours old, so seals can give birth in estuaries when sandbanks are exposed or on rocky shores between tides.

In clear waters a seal uses its eye-sight to hunt for shellfish and sand eels, but in the murkier depths it sweeps its head to and fro, feeling for food with its long, coarse whiskers.

*Grey seal*

# Our Marine Heritage

**As mentioned in the introduction to this booklet, many of the amazing species found in our seas and around our coasts are protected under the European Habitats Directive, launched as a result of the Rio Earth Summit in 1992.**

To help the UK put the Directive into practice, the UK Marine SACs LIFE Project was founded. It involved a 5-year partnership between the European Union LIFE funding agency, the UK conservation agencies and the Scottish Association of Marine Science.

The project has gathered a great wealth of knowledge and understanding from people across the whole of the UK. This has helped us to take the needs of people into account while conserving our marine biodiversity.

Much of our wildlife and natural habitats can be sustained alongside human activities. In fact, the sustainable management of our European marine sites will be successful only with the co-operation and commitment of those who live, work, or spend their leisure time in and around these sites.

Five years ago, the UK and the rest of Europe had relatively little experience of protecting marine wildlife. Now we can be confident about what can be achieved for marine conservation, strengthened by our increased knowledge and valuable new partnerships.

This booklet is one of the many achievements of the UK Marine SACs LIFE project. Further information on the project and the Habitats Directive in the UK can be found at:

www.ukmarinesacs.org.uk
www.snh.org.uk
www.ccw.gov.uk
www.english-nature.org.uk
www.ehsni.gov.uk
www.jncc.gov.uk
www.sams.ac.uk